The Me Theme

Doug Nufer

© 2017 by Doug Nufer
Book design © 2017 by Sagging Meniscus Press

All Rights Reserved.

Printed in the United States of America.
Set in Van Dijck MT with LaTeX.

ISBN: 978-1-944697-42-6 (paperback)
ISBN: 978-1-944697-43-3 (ebook)
Library of Congress Control Number: 2017934440

Sagging Meniscus Press
web: http://www.saggingmeniscus.com/
email: info@saggingmeniscus.com

Why is justice just ice?

—Chris Toll

to a dear toad ear shell
a corresponsive lyric halo of shellac
or responsively rich aloof lo-tech lot echo
verse arches over searches
recalled, re-called

O pen, open an aesthetic anaesthetic tome to me.
Revising rev, I sing amused, am used to no meter tonometer
Human hum, an ideal I deal, parsing par, sing the me theme.

The Me Theme

Contents Con Tents

I'm a Gist Imagist	1
News and New Sand	13
Con Science Conscience	21
Recreation Re-creation	35
In Foreign Info Reign	39
Rum or Rumor	51
Your Yo Ur, The Sis Thesis	55
Writ, He'd Writhed	65
We Were Readying a Dying Ozone O Zone	77
Mythic Kaleidoscope, My Thick Ale I Do Scope	87
Fatalist's Fat A-Lists	95
The REM in Theremin	109
All Us I've Allusively Lyre Recited, Cited	117
Fare Well, Farewell	121

I'm a Gist Imagist

Just ice justice, reinstate rein
State the me theme
Factor fact or temper
A mental temperamental
Leg end legend.

Mistrust mist, rust art if ice,
Artifice restrains rest
Rains beat.

Be at bat on baton
Wag on wagon auto mated car, a van
Automated caravan assembling
As sembling per uses
Illiterate peruses.

I'll iterate the me theme
Just ices justice's den.

I, Zen denizen,
Am using amusing cons
Trained constrained
Imbedding I'm bedding.

Polyphilia is on
Polyp hi liaison,
A basing abasing
Onsets on sets.

I'm a gist imagist
A polo gist apologist, a
Bashed abashed agent, a gent
Attesting at testing
Artichoke art
I choke
Anthems, ant hems

Poe try poetry
Port rayed portrayed temperas
Temp eras formats for mats.
Rampages ramp ages ram pages.

For the forth emerged merged
Meantime me/anti-me meant
I'm easy as yearning
Earning some ideal tome.

So, me I deal to me,
Mean me, an ivied I, vied.

My co-logical mycological
My O sis myosis the sis thesis mythic alchemist
Mythical chemist Medea me
DEA me
A Dow napalm's meadow nap.

Alms-meager me,
Ager me, a sled measled meat.

Me at medial me
Dial me, Doc Medoc.

Meet me, ET.

Me, gap hone megaphone megaspore me
Gas pore megapode me gap ode.

Me gat here megathere me gat on megaton.

Meiosis me I O sis melee me lee melodeon me lode on
Me men to memento.

I'm a Gist Imagist

Me no pause menopause, me rely merely, meshy
Me shy mesoblast me sob last mesocratic me
Socratic me son meson methane me thane.

Me tier metier metonym
Me to nym me
Me meme

Taxi tax I:
Impost or impostor,
I'm post or pole mic polemic
To pony my toponymy bull
Slinger cowboys.

Bulls linger, cow boys, menace men.
Ace nib licks niblicks chip per
Chipper parameter par.
A meter line age lineage
Assigns as signs post script.

Postscript addenda add, end a letter
Man letterman jockeyed jock-eyed
Side-saddle sides, addle forth
Right forthright
Realist A-list sincere since mania's man, I,
As the me theme in auger at or
Inaugurator rearranging rear
Ranging back wards backwards.

Backwards wards back ranging
Rear rearranging inaugurator,
Or at augur in theme me the as I,
Man mania's since sincere A-list realist
forthright, right, forth
Addle sides side-saddle

I'm a Gist Imagist

Jock-eyed jockeyed letterman man letter A,
End, add addenda postscript script.

Post signs as assigns lineage
Age line meter a par parameter
Chipper per chip niblicks licks nib.

Ace men menace boys, cow, linger.
Bulls cowboys,
Slinger bull toponomy my pony to
Polemic mic pole or post,
I'm impostor or impost
I tax taxi.

I mouth
I'm out-howled.

Owl Edens ensconce conceits?
It's Babylon, baby.
Lonely Elysée?
See solipsism.

So lips, I, SM-averse, suckled
A verse suck, led my threadbare myth.

Read bare, win
Some winsome thesis.

The sis might yoke
Mighty O.K. ear arias.

I ascertain certain landau land
Aura rapt ole man Ptolemanias.

I assume Sumerian-riant tokens
O.K. ensconsing cons in
Gaffable affable bro brogan
Ganef-effacing facing
Clodhopper clod hop per
The me theme lean
To lean-to fort
Reason for treason.

Betrayed psychological bet
Rayed psycho? Logical?
Ill-bet, hear, biter?

O, fall
I'll be the arbiter of all.

I nap.
Prehension, inapprehension itself
Its elf fun dreams fund reams,
Paperweight Pa,
Per weight.

I've erred, I veer red, asleep
As lee placed laced fillagreed fill.

A greed for ego esteeming
Foregoes teeming reflexive reflex.

I've wallowed.
Wall owed fort
Nights fortnights
Lay over layover
Of flights off lights
Sot ethers
So tethers snap
Drag on snapdragon
Turn ipso facto
Turnip so fact,
O napiform nap I form
Eggplant's egg

Plants heat
Hen heathen.
Don't hatch, don thatch
Fleetingly flee tingly dungeons dung.

I'm a Gist Imagist

Eons inestimable,
I nest, I'm able as a plucky a sap lucky bull dozing
Bulldozing to praise top, raise
The Sis Thesis feathers'
Feat, hers.

Iridescent, I ride scent.
I on one ionone odor OD
Or haddock chowder ring do soup
Had dock chow derring-do so up-chuck
Wag on chuck wagon rotor rot.

Or
I o none
I on one
Ionone
Ion one aroma
A Roma bella donna belladonna
Nights Hades nightshades infuse.

In fuse litmus kerosene
My lit musk
Eros enemy comedies come,
Die, smell.

I, fluent mellifluent, weave.

We ave perfumes
Per fume's hand
I cap, handicap star charts, starch arts,
Boss on ovarian arrow
Bossonova narrow gig
O lo gigolo ax is X-rated if ice
Axis X rat edifice chore
O graph Y choreography.

News and New Sand

War bled, warbled
The sis thesis sag, a saga
Assignation ass.

I, gnat,
I on pushover pus
Hover, push over Cialis

So me, CIA lissome, xy lop
Honed xylophoned scala wags.

Scalawags dish on
Or dishonor gent eel.

Genteel, I'm a GI nation
Imagination sold, i.e.
Ring soldiering circled jerk
In circ-led jerkin uniform.

UN, I form cordon cord
On combat comb
At pompadour pomp
A dour fragrant frag rant.

Heartily, he artily foraged
For aged romantic
Roman tic to gated togated
Epicenter epic enter fanfares.

Fan fares seethe,
See the onus on us.

Properties' proper ties
Swam pedigreed.

Swamped, I greedy,
Am mercantile.

Yammer can tile, show
Erst all shower stall cleansing clean,
Sing slogans, slog.

Answering, we ringmasters of tent ozone
Master, soften to zone tar pits as parks.

Tarp, it's a spark's kindling.
Kind lingo oars on shell skipper
Arson's hell, skip permit tsar mitts,
Arrest rest.

Lessor less or a lien germ,
An alien German inhabits a loft
In habits aloft, toadying to a dying
Superintendent's notice to be gone.

Super in ten dent snot ice to beg
On evict or victorious,
I oust rusty trusty
Do or man doorman vigil antes.

Vigilantes' proper ties
Properties we rent.

Weren't we weasling a sling
Release re: lease brokerings?
Broke rings sue suede
Decadence cadence.

News and New Sand

Sentries, sen tries go on;
Goon doyens
Do yen's investments.

In vestments, Pa trolled
Patrolled pat rolled
Reconversion recon version
Restore rest ore lotto lot to Vatican vat.

I can gainsay gain
Say veins tone.

Veinstone ordeal or deal
Double-down doubled
Own a gate agate
For mica Formica.

My sore Mysore swami swam
In olive stocks, no livestocks
Ruby rub yogi ogive,
Vesting stingy escrows.

Yes, crows rob or rant
Roborant to niche tonic;
He reapportions reap portions
Lotto lot to investments
In vestments dominus do minus dom in us.

Tabus tab us
Jujube juju behind us Hindus
Don key donkey blanket
Blank ethereality.
He, reality bum per rein car nates'
Bumper, reincarnates heretics,
Here tics, as pirated aspirated
Bib list Biblist Fundamentalists.

Fund a mentalist's
Imp act impact
Toward to ward off end offend,
"I slam Islam!"

No vice novice, I, nun, dated
Inundated Papal Pa pal
Sodomy bullet in.

So do my bulletin pulpits pulp
Its yellow newsprint?

Yell ow!
New sprint parade relic tapes,
Par a derelict, ape spraying praying
Theanthropic rumor.

The anthropic rum or
Firewater fire waterproof proof
Wit chalices witch Alices

Go ogle Google
To read or surf
Ace toreador surface pieties.

Shoo-fly pie ties shoo
Fly in tole rant intolerant
Blithe ring blithering.

Form any juris dictions
For many jurisdictions.

Garbage's garb ages the me theme
Best robed bestrobed

Hung, owned, hun-gowned fat
Her father icons train

I constrain form albums formal bums
Preen acted preenacted pageants
Page ants ascents as cents in jury injury.

Primal outlaw, prim,
A lout law student stud
Entangled angled
But tonsure button sure balderdash
Balder dash bigwigs wired rugs
Big wigs wire drugs.

Poppy cocks poppycock's crossbow
Cross-bow fire shot
Fires hot claptraps clap
Traps driveled drive-led garb age garbage
For many form any
Juris dictions jurisdictions.

Con Science Conscience

The saurus thesaurus shallowing shall
Owing to taxonomy
Tax on (O my),
Assay as say
Behemoths be
He moths
Butterflies.

Butter flies up holstered
Gats by upholstered
Gatsby armchair
Arm chairmen acing menacing
Zoometric zoo metric
Revenue re venue.

Bandits band its
Withdrawing with drawing panorama
Pan O ram a cartoon car
To on-par.

A taxi's parataxis par a tax is
Nowhere now herefor
For the IRS, theirs.

The sis thesis chicken
Chic Ken, part he,
No gene sis
Parthenogenesis petri puppet.

Pet, rip up petroleum role
Umbras bras barb, i.e. Barbie.

Doll operas, dollop eras
Investigated ashes.

Cortices invest?
I gate dash.

Escort, I,
Cestus tush hoverer
Over erotic otic
Ya-ya yahoo hoopla
Plastic Ken stick encores
Core-sample ample
Mother lo desire.

Motherlode sire,
Manakin man
Akin an atom icon anatomic
Onus probandi (us pro-ban diagnostics agnostics
In deco rum indecorum disco untamed) discount.

A mediated I
At edgy gyno nosy synestheia nest:
He, I, a broken bro Ken,
O, be, obey estrous, yes
Trouser vice service.

I slander islander eremites
Ere mites cross hairs.

Crosshairs zoom aim
Zoo-maiming ingrate, rate panaceas
Pan a ceased edema
Emanation nation,
A toll atoll booth eel boot heel.
Boo the elfish fish islander.

I slander vertigo
Vert? I go chartreuse
Chart re-use, so fade coraliferous
Sofa decor, a life roustabouts tab
Outside ideal albatross bat.

Ross Sea seared red
For cerise's force rises.

Arch, I pelagic, archipelagic seaman seam,
An officer off icer quack salve
Regrets quacksalver egrets
Ingest, in Gestapo apocryphal cry,
Phallic licorice or ice.

I so bar
Isobar weather balloon
We at herbal loon
Inversions in versions atone.

At one A tone
The me theme harmonizes.

Harm on, I zest ironist, stir on.
I strain Rainier's rainier sis train:
I strain rain gutter gut terminuses.

Minuses incur rents
In currents, tradewind upshots
Trade wind-ups, hot tarp, its
Tar pit's La Brea thing:
L.A. breathing.

Isodiametric I
Sod I a metric isogamete
I sog a mete isogamy.

I, so gamy
I sog Amy.

I so gloss isogloss
I sog loss.

I so gram
I sog
Ram isogram.

I so late isolate I;
Some try isometry.

I, son
O my
I so
No my isonomy
I sop OD.

Isopod is
O pod isostatic.
I, so static, I, so there is
O there I
Sot, here isothere isotonic.

I so tonic isotope, I, sot
Ope isotropic I so tropic.

I vied ivied to a sty
Ale toast Yale:
Boo lab oo la boola.

I'm a go met, am Orphic
Imago metamorphic insect
In sect love done loved one
Cater pillar caterpillar
Butterfly butter.

Fly, pup pupa.
Alar larva vagrant,
Grant rest.

Orations, restorations, alterations
Alte rations highlight high, lightsome
So mesothoraces sot ho
Races Ovid, Eos.

O videos, photos hop, photoshop
So metamorphism, tam Orphism, adult,
Adulterate era tegument gum entomologists.

O mol O gists
Molecule mole culex X-ray
Rayon ondogram, do gram
Masses' hot masse shot
Beacon version
Be a conversion.

Isinglass is in glass
I sin glass I sing lass
Isinglass gelatin gel
A tin gel at in
Shimmy shim my
Stand-offish stand of fish.

Amalfi a mal fishy sterno shyster
No Med, I terrane animal Mediterranean
I'm alive, I've tuna tun, a
Put rid per fumes putrid perfumes
Pro ducts products convey.

Or conveyor line
Manacling lineman, a cling
Can til ever cantilever
Bowfin germane sashimi.

Bow finger, mane sash, I'm, I avow,
A vowel elbowing bowing icons on
Antic consonant iced edge genotypes.

No types skip jack's skipjacks
Bill fish billfish lampreys
Lam preys high way menacing highwaymen
Acing outdoor outdo or see sawfish.

See-saw fish decor ate dinner,
Decorated inner sewages sea monster no
Sew ages seam on sterno rest
Itches, restitches.

The me theme radioactive radio act
I've tuned in tune din den dense
Semi-misc. sci-fi,
If I may hem mayhem to wed, towed
Fact or factorial I
Alias I as
In to-to into
Total tallying lying myth,
My thought ought meander me
And ergo go.

Radiation's rad I at ions
Literal arm lit, ER alarm cat scan cats,
Can can certain cancer
Tainted eddying, dying.

"Mekong me, Kong, fu kush?
I'm a Fukushima sore actor
Rodan, so react or reactor rod
An unrestraining unrest raining stun
Grays stung rays,"

Big Sur faced big surf;
Aced waves hocked
Wave-shocked westward ho tsunami.

West ward hot sun.
Am I Godzilla's god Z?

Con Science Conscience

I'll as uranium ur
An I umpyre pyre kindled
Kind-led conflagration
Con flag ration isotopic
Allied mendacity.

I, so topical, lied,
"Mend a city atomically, atomic ally."

Recreation Re-creation

Measure me
A sure Everest eve rest
Bedlam bed lamp
It on piton rig
Or rigor now here
No, where real tors realtors
Areas are as gigantic
Gig antic limbs.

Anti-climbs rappel, rap
Pellucid pale or arete nets
Lucid paleo rare tenets
Con, descending
Condescending amounts recount
A mount's recount, amass a massif
If my thin stanced
Myth-instanced egg,
e.g. golden olden omen.

O, men go
At goat rib bonuses, ribbon uses
To taled beanstalk totaled
Beans talk fief of, um
"Fie fo fum."

Recreation Re-creation

Broglio, Ma, for Brock?
Bro, glioma forb rock?

Man agers managers, human,
Hum an imbroglio: I'm Broglio,
Cubbyholed Cub by holed card in also
Cardinal so coinsure coin sure Brock ages
Brockages pat in a patina hard ball.

Hardball legend leg end
He artily heartily can, did
Candid stealthy steal thy assets
As sets retired re:
Tired arm or armor
A gain's tan
Against an
Imbroglio?

I'm Broglio, infamous
In famous trade
Marked trademarked.

Impressed? I'm pressed to win, tow in;
Am bit: I on ambition box.

Cartouches boxcar touchés cart ridgepole in tent
Cartridge intent, polemic microwaves row.

A vespine swarm pines warm for bidding
Forbidding sting, stingy yet etherizing her;
I zing her, her ring herring, my O Ma,
Myoma tumor, tum or do ominous doom.

I? No, us roustabouts roust a bout's
Koala K.O., a la marsupial low, mars;
Up I allow, intending in tending
Loves gloves.

Punches pun chesty, stymy my arm
Aged Don.

Armageddon,
Usher us, her
Bringing herb
Ringing a numb ere now often
A number enow of ten count
Down countdown.

In Foreign Info Reign

✺ Yakima yak? I'm a Tacoma taco Ma, yum.
A Yuma par is Paris sand
I, ego San Diego, tamp.

A Tampa Rom a Roma bar
Row Barrow tor
On to Toronto.

Pensacola pens a cola
Or leans Orleans wall a wall a Walla Walla
Victoria victor.

I, a Marin mar in re: no Reno
Nor folk Norfolk
Stock ton Stockton day ton
A Daytona C-level and Cleveland
Cash mere Cashmere red ding.

Redding band on Bandon reed
Sport Reedsport Logan log
An Elma elm a belling ham Bellingham.

Chic ago, Chicago ran goon Rangoon crime;
A Crimea Jackson jacks on war
Saw Warsaw tole do Toledo mad
Rid Madrid, man a squan Manasquan son
Or a Sonora Manhattan man hat
An Athens at hens washing ton Washington bud

In Foreign Info Reign

A pest Budapest Dunedin dune din sing a pore Singapore
As wan Aswan Hanoi?

Ha, no I be I
Rut Beirut, nag a saki
Nagasaki rotter, dam Rotterdam liver,
Pool Liverpool bright on Brighton.
Tunis tun is my sore Mysore Pullman pull man Galway
      gal way
Bangalore, ban gal ore bang a lore ban galore

✳ Is ISIS Isis?
I saw ere awe recalling whoever lastingly
calling who everlastingly
Isis is.

Is the sis thesis Theban?
The ban on an Onan is.
Is Isis Theban?

The ban, Theban,
O, sir is Osiris
On an Onan cult
Us cultus
Menispermaceous men,
I spermaceous, guy,
Wired guywired
To get her.

Together, we'd ding
Wedding bellowed bell owed
Panther pant
Her catalog cat
A log jam boree jamboree
The sis thesis inspires.

In spires' humbugs
Hum bugs' anthems
Ant hems tailor tail
Or rest, itch, restitch

The be Thebe motto mot to
Raising Ra I sing.

So, we to Soweto came 'roun' Cameroun
To go install Togo in stall a frican
Madagascar African mad
A gas car so Mali a Somalia
Gab on Gabon zooid zoo.

I'd led a Leda anile, a Nile swan as wan
Aswan Dam aged, damaged
The ban Theban authorities
Author I, ties wore, swore.

❋ I ran Iran
Asia Minor, as I am
In or Outer Mongolia.
Ou? Term on gol
I an ether, lands
Netherlands net
Her lands.

Ireland ire, land Germany germ any
Poland pol and Cuba cub a den mark.

Denmark mad
A gas car Madagascar
Spa in Spain.

Pan a ma
Panama guy, an A
Guyana Afghan.

Is tan Afghanistan
Tim or Timor
And or Ra Andorra sum
At era Sumatera?

Argentina argent in a
Malaysia
Ma lays.

I, a Yemen ye men
Oman O man bot swan,

In Foreign Info Reign

A Botswana Mexico me X,
I co-chin a China Aden, a den
Norway nor way to go
Togo can a DA Canada malt
A Malta Algeria Alger, I, a Hun Gary
Hungary dom in a can Dominican.

Bonuses bon uses jet aim emission
Je t'aime, Miss, I on mission mon amour.

Mona Mo
Ur maman mam
An à demain ade ma
In Paris par is me, moi
R memoir rendition.

Rend it
I on le vin levin
Je suis Jesu.

Is mon sacré mons
Acre mon sac
Re la passion?
Lap ass.

I, on Mont Age
Montage amour
Am our savior-faire savior.

Fa ire chantage
Chant age nous
No us pen sons
Pensons que … enchanter
Queen Chant, er, royale

In Foreign Info Reign

Roy Ale can can can-can
Pot able potable sanglots sang
Lots de vin et devine
Tapage à page.

✳︎   Sampling's Sam
Plings indifference.

In difference apart
A part I'm proving
Improving Shinto shin to doyens.

Do yens
For tune fortune cookie cook i.e.
Chefoo Chef Oo
Mess aged messaged mass ages massages
Rub blessed rubble's sediment?

I'm entrapping rapping
Crumbles.

Sons' crumb lessons off laws of flaws
Imparted imp-arted proverbs.

Pro verbs mingled Ming, led
Vase line vaseline:

Be at beat to win assets, tow in
As sets: win now.

Winnow the me theme
Anear an ear.

Co-defend code
Fend the me theme
Code X codex code.

Co-delegate legate,
His panic Hispanic
Lamp ray slam prays
No, blesses noblesses,

"May a Maya culpa
Bled culpable display
I splay is play surgeon."

Surge once notes
Cenotes' tomb oyster
Tomboy sternum numskulls.

Skulls mandate man, date attendance
At ten dance hall owed hallowed sac
Redly sacredly barbecued bar.

Be cued, conquest.
Con quest fronteras
Front eras span.

I, ardent Spaniard, entwine
Wine slurp eons slur peons
Pint a Pinta to Nina
Toniná piñata
Pin at a cantina
Cant in a barcarole Barça role bar car olé.

Rum or Rumor

Itinerate,
I tine rate, forking
For king's tabled stabled
Stab-led assassin's ass
As sins endanger.

End anger
Alter native alternative nostrums
No strums strum.

Pet strumpet Cupid cup
I'd go sling gosling goo
Sing goosing rump.

Us rumpus rumor rum or
Nog gin noggin
Barflies barf lies,
Determine, deter, mine
Dramamine's drama mines.

Sodapop? Sod!
A pop port unity
Opportunity.

Cove rage coverage imports
I'm port's Dow.

Agers, dowagers sip, hon
Siphon Ruinart, ruin art aspiration
As pi ration mathematic Ma thematic
Seersuckers-wearing seer sucker
Swearing suitor suit
Or high, highjack.

Screw jacks crew
Who're whores ailing, sailing
Aboard a board ketch
Up-swilling ketch-up's willing
Catsup cats up tippled tip-pled
Grogram grog, Ram brand, is
Bran dis tilled distilled.

Wassailing was sailing
Teetotaling? Tee totaling's mashed
Smashed.

Insipid in sip
I'd in hale inhale
Gas con ade's gasconades.

The me theme assistance ass, I,
Stance inflated in flat Edda daring,
Ring freed rinks around
Free drinks, a round
Increased in creased pantaloons.

Pant a loon's bill owed billowed
Pain staking painstaking
Gassings gas sings boastingly.

Boas tingly constrictor con strict
Orbiting, biting asp ires
Aspires call.

I, graphic alky jelly shooter
Calligraphical KY jelly's hooter
Under line underline underlying
Under lying cursive curs I've fed.

Or a fedora wearing
Sinatra temp led sin
At Ra templed jujube
Camel absolutions
Juju became
Lab solutions.

Your Yo Ur, The Sis Thesis

The me theme thesis the sis thearchies
The Archies
Arose a rose tour
To ur menace men.

Ace wombat womb at comb at combat
To Ma hawk tomahawk roust
A bout male diction.

Roustabout malediction
Managing man
Aging xy
Loses xylose's wooden woo den rigor.

Pantiewaists rig or pan, tie waists, seed ire
See dire backslashing.

Backs lashing whipper-snappers whip
Per snappers flagrant flag rant.

Patriots, pat riots,
Padrones Pa drones
Rave?

No
Us ravenous
Menus men us
Diner diners

Up sup ours
O ur
Smotherings motherings.

❋   Art is an artisan shaman sham
An artifact art
If act
Art I fact check
Books, checkbooks.

Many earned man yearned
Seethings.

See things, passion pass
I on origins
(or I, gins
Ingest in gest).

Textiled text, I led
Inciting in citing sources, spools
Sour cesspools.

So, ur gently, so urgently
Sour gent lyres rescue, cue
Leaden lea den run grounds
Rung rounds
As A's orchestrate Chopin.

Or chest rate chop
In hearts he arts beat
Be at me at meat mete
Or meteor cratered crate red pit
A pat pitapat be at beat.

Your Yo Ur, The Sis Thesis

Mime sis mimesis
Or gang rind
Errant organ grinder
Rant cantor
Cant or mummer chant mum
Merchant rabbitry.

Rabbi, try ham,
Let hamlet bumpkins
Bump kins.

Incest in
Ces't-a-dire
A dire strait straitjacket
Jack ethic hiccups, cups
The sis thesis bromides bro,
Mid-estrus trussings,
Sings in cites incites cultural cult
Ural-influent main stream
In fluent mainstream flux.

Us Fluxus recon nectar rivals
Reconnect arrivals to a sting,
Toasting:

"The sis thesis
Mode sty modesty
Pries tupping priest
Upping sodomists."

So do mists infest:
I've heaven on ego;
In festive heave,
None go.

Your Yo Ur, The Sis Thesis

Conception concept, I on infancy in, fancy a slip
As lip afoot a foot shin, dig the sis shindig thesis
Top résumé to presume form, ally formally
Off-limits of flim-its-flam in goading us.

Flamingo, a dingus of fens,
I've offensively lysed sedimentally.

I, men tally,
Made faces.

Ma defaces my co-sis mycosis fungus fun gusto
To generate gene rate pay in gland paying landlady
Ladybug bugbears, bears fruit.

I, on fruition
Lunging lung ingest
Estrayed rayed be a Ms. beams.

Hogshead hogs head headlines head lines, bar barm;
Awful maw fulfilling filling cask, etch casket chance ancestor storages,
A gesture tureens ensnare.

Nares not snot holes, tholes, or phantom bayou orphan tomb,
A you limbo, die slim; bodies go.

A lie goal, i.e. lotto lot to ascribe,
A scribe's wampum swamp umbones bones
Replay rep, lay my larghetto mylar ghetto internment.

Intern mentors or surgeons urge onslaught laughter;
Eristic, I stick kaput, a putrid riddance dance cad, aver
Cadaver, scar Cassandra's carcass
And rain in ashes as she's presentimentally present.

I, mentally done, do need edits; its tapes
Try tapestry for mending form ending.

Your Yo Ur, The Sis Thesis

The sis thesis beauties' beau tie slips,
Lips part ridges
Partridges bob white.

Bobwhite quails quail, surrendering ur
Rendering some retreats
So mere treats for ego forego
Hi-fi shy, hi-fishy gatherings.

Gat he-rings, ganglions
Gang lions den I-grating
Denigrating con stabled cons
Tabled constabled beat tractions.

Be attraction's pint-ailed pintailed ducklings,
Duck ling's seas on season, celebrate.

Celeb rate, the me theme beauties' beau
Ties his sing-hissing asp
Halt asphalt jungled Jung.

Led awry, a wry mobster mobs sterile ileitis
It is inflamed in flamed marshmallowed
Marsh mall owed in test in allocating
Intestinal locating anent rails.

An entrails gut gutter terrace race
Hands Omega, Ga.

Handsome gag a hand
Some gaga Adonis.

A don is Oxford's ox, Ford's
Mad Ox Ford Madox Ford.

Writ, He'd Writhed

So, me?
Some overweening over weening author,
I tar. I, an authoritarian prick,
Led prickled book keepers
Bookkeepers,
Off ice office
Red actors, redactors
A gent's agents
Copyright copy right about rightabout trademarkers
Trade markers celebrating celeb rating pop corn
Popcorn gobbling gob bling admirers
Ad mirers
Typo graphic sex tantamount sextant amount
       typographic font
Allayers fontal layers forest all forestall imprints.
I'm print's artifact or artifactor
Art I factor.

Writ, He'd Writhed

Am I no amino compass?
I, on compassion
Generally gene rally
My otic, myotic handicap.

Hand, I cap appendages
Append ages' era sure erasure capacity
Cap a city chromo
Some chromosome
Chic ago Chicago sand burg
Sandburg invented.

In vented cornices
Corn ices woolens.

Woo lens? My otic myotic
Compassion compass
I on watchman watch
Man a sextant
As extant a band on
Abandon as sent
Assent conducts our conduct sour.

✲ Do geared down Beats
Dog-eared downbeats
Re-amuse, ream
Use the me theme?

Ginsberg's gins
Berg smelts melt snot
Iced noticed
How lingo in Howl
In going
Races.

Graces have no haven?
Ow! Hitman Whitman,
Likewise, like, wisely lyrical,

I calamity amity am I
Typed pederast?

Eras tab abuse, use
Some so-so me's, O, He:
Romantic hero man
Ticking off king officers
Icers, vices' quadrant
Vice squad rant closet omens
Close to mens rumor
Rum or gins, bergs
Ginsberg's cock, tails
Cocktails.

Hum Bly humbly.

His Tory history withering wit
He ring rankled rank-led men.

Ace menace
Pre-enacted preen-acted peacock
Pea cock bump ride bum pride.

As pirate aspirate
Scab bards scabbards
Handle, bar handlebar mustache,
Must ache.

Man
I fold manifold
Humbly hum Bly.

Poe tics poetics pit a pat pitapat
Pen dent pendent raven
O us ravenous rave
Nevermore raven ever.

Moreover overtoney toney tonometers
To no meterstick stickler.

Le roi? Oiling lingoes
O, esteeming teeming arenas
Are nasty tyrants' rants
Peaking speaking soliloquies
So lil O quiescent central rales
Escaped caped lunging lung.

Ingrate, rate amid as a Midas,
I touch it, ouch!

A do be adobe gold brickyard bug led
Arm goldbrick yard bugled armpit bull.

Pitbull stubborn stub, born short
Changing short-changing
Withstanding with standing coinage
Coin a gestate state
Pal ace palace coup
On coupon
Usher us her, Lenore,
Le nor'easter aster
The sea city's cape
Cityscape.

Workshop works hop
Prosecutor prose cut, or in verse,
Inverse per verse perverse
Span king-spanking cognomen cog
No men man.

Drills, mandrills
Rearrange rear range me men to
Memento assembling as sembling humbug
Hum bug sonnets
(son nets the sis thesis rave led, raveled).

Revise re: vise,
Reinvent rein, vent
Attic kingdom I nations
At ticking dominations
Foraged for aged
Night ropes nigh tropes
Post master postmaster-buttondown butt
On down home O static homeostatic
Patina pat in a wooden woo den
With drawn withdrawn caveat cave
At col lapses collapses.

Pendent pen, dent
Stymy sty my penitentiaries.
Penitent I, Aries, ramble
Ram bleat at sin
Us sinus hanky pan kyack
Hanky-panky acknowledges.

Now ledges imply I'm
Plymouth Rock's tar mouth rock star
Whose dated solo wails
Who sedated so low ails
In undated inundated
Floodplain songs.

Flood plainsongs
Sandbag sand, bags, and traps, sandtraps
Hooting trapshooting marksman, marks
Man noticed.

Not iced, rube factions
Rubefactions redistrict red.

I, strict pen, non pennon standard or banner vier,
Stand ardor, ban nervier pens I've, pensive red acted,
Redacted Pa limp: sestina palimpsest in a
Form a list formalist beef
Arts bee farts.

Writ, He'd Writhed

Miss I on mission alien a lien
Together to get her ragout rag out
Investment sin vestments amass a mass
For raging foraging forbear for bear
Assisting ass I sting abet a bet
In foreign info reign again a gain

The rapist therapist again a gain
A goon ago on alien a lien
Entrances entrances abet a bet
No vices novices ragout rag out
Revising rev I sing forbear for bear
Traps hooting trap-shooting amass a mass

For tuna Fortuna amass a mass
Just ices justices again a gain
Do wagers' dowagers forbear for bear
Pass I on passion alien a lien
Dishearten, dish ear ten ragout rag out
But tresses buttresses abet a bet

Addictions, ad dictions abet a bet
Temp tingly temptingly amass a mass
Monsignored mons ignored ragout rag out
Lit any litany again a gain
Outdo or outdoor alien a lien
Restraint, O rest rain to forbear for bear

In no cents innocents forbear for bear
Impostor impost or abet a bet
To seethe to see the alien a lien
Endorsing end or sing amass a mass
Allowing all, O wing again a gain
Contract or contractor ragout rag out

Discouraged disc, our aged ragout rag out
In fan try infantry forbear for bear
Bombastic bomb as tic again a gain
Advisor sad visors abet a bet
Off ices offices amass a mass
Forego for ego alien a lien

Ragout rag out alien a lien again a gain
Forbear for bear amass a mass
A gain again ragout rag out abet a bet.

Writ, He'd Writhed

Sonnets' son nets his tone
Histone glob in globin substances
Sub stances, subversing sub
Versing iambic pentameters.

"I am Bic pent, a meter's writ,"
He'd writhed anti crimes
Antic rimes applying
App lying easeled ease.

Led by line by-line
Contradictions contra diction's
Noun, no unadvised
Ad-vised clam per clamper
Can dent candent lam plight
Lamplight shadowing shad
Owing sonnets son nets.

Prodigious pro, dig IOUs' sweepstake
Sweeps take abundances. A bun dance's
I'm passively impassively to do,
To-do aside, a side in sensitive
Insensitive to, O, so on too soon.
But tresses buttresses panache pan ache
Dishonoring dish on O-ring fortunes
For tunes I'm posed imposed a sis as is
Thematically the Ma tic ally pen
Is penis thesis tome: the sis to me
Bestowed. Best owed, rep aid repaid again
A gain icon iconographically
O graphically with drawn withdrawn per use
Peruse prodigious pro dig IOUs.

We Were Readying a Dying Ozone O Zone

※   We arable wearable fields
　　Toned rugged fieldstone
　　Drugged landscaper lands caper
　　Tu lips pouting
　　Tulip-spouting
　　Chummy chum
　　My top-soil tops oil steelheads
　　Steel heads per chances perch.

　　Ancestries' tries fallowed
　　Fall owed me a dowl ark's
　　Meadowlarks catbird seat.

　　Cat birds eat, hawking.
　　Haw king ox end rovers
　　Oxen drovers rut a bag
　　A rutabaga rut in rutin
　　Buckwheat buck wheat.

Were wolves
Werewolves
Howling how ling cod
A coda fin ale
Finale swam?

I, swami, a vat ars avatar's
Manifest man, if estranged, ranged.

I'm proving improving me
A sly me
Measly lycanthrope can thro'
Peruses ruses believe belie velure
Lure ga-ga Gaza Zazu Zulu
Lupine pineal alpha phase semen men.

Menacmes men acmes met
A mere metamere, a somite's
As, O, mites in fest infest packs,
Addled packsaddled quadra/biped
Qua drab I peduncles uncles.

Stalking stalk ingravescent
Rave scent illness,
I'll Ness Loch lochia
(I a monster mons termagant
A gantlet) let my mythic
Thick kinky inky id

Entity Identity bay, oust
Bayou strolling rolling quick
Silver bullet in quicksilver bulletin.

We Were Readying a Dying Ozone O Zone

"We stern western sheriffs,"
She riffs, a hi-fi tine rant not ice ah if itinerant notice
"Aren't a rent strike outlaw sin."

Strike-out laws, insult
Ultra trail illustrated lust rated
Rodeos rod.

Eos? She'd shed Ponderosas,
Ponder O sashay hay rollings
Tone rolling.

Stoned rovers, drovers
Stamp, stampede Eden.

"Ascent nascent, tee the Dawn,
Teethed awn in grain awning rain."
Torn ados, tornados rear
Range in dust rialto
Rearrange industrial totem templates.

Plates rush more Rushmore figureheads
Figure headstone to near tone-arm overage,
Move rage, turn tables turntables.

Disc avenged, I scavenge.

❋ The me theme concupiscent con cup
Is cent scenting ingot!

Otiose I, O securing curing
Spendthrift, spend.

Thrift is sued
Issued, overblown:
Lipservice.

Over blown lip service
Weathers trip.

We, at her strip teasing tea,
Sing for giving forgiving
Misspent housepet Miss Penthouse Pet,
Her ovary hero.

Vary pleasure,
Plea? Sure.
Pleas urethra thrasonical sonic alarms arm
Smug mug student stud enticers.

Icers, I recount ire count
Innocents in no cents
Pending spending.

We Were Readying a Dying Ozone O Zone

We, although wealth ought tether ether,
Farther fart heritages.

It ages us using
Ingredient red,
I entrust: rust.

Cap era, caper a city's cape
Cityscape scrim. I, no logical criminological
Gumshoe gums.

Hoedown downtown tow nabobs
A bobsled ledger geranium, an I,
Umpired pi, redistributed rip-off
Underwriter slush reappraising.

Is tribute, drip of funder writers' lush reap,
Praising wretched wretch edacity?

A citystate statement or mentor pronouncement
Pronoun cement per se cured per secured areas.

Are assets sets improvised?
I'm pro-vised clamped clam
Pedantic antic banking.

Ban king succession,
Success I once ceded, deducted.

Ducted, I taped it
Aped pipe dreams
Piped reams we evil weevil
Insects in fest in sects infest.

We Were Readying a Dying Ozone O Zone

We were readying
A dying Ozone Oz
One O Zone

So me, where
Somewhere over, overt here re:
The rainbow rain bowl

Ingle ague bowling league
Revel at ions revelations
Borealis bore a lispendens
Pen density.

I, tycoon coonhound,
Hound takeovers.

Take overshades Hades
Imposing doom ensigns
I'm posing: do omen signs fail?

Safe, fail-safe, we—
We're replying plyings pray, can
Spraycan ozone Oz One O Zone.

*Mythic Kaleidoscope, My Thick Ale
I Do Scope*

Gemini gem in
I, Castor, cast
Or Pollux pol lux
United unit, edit it,
The real of there aloft.

The aterminus theater
Minus side,
Real sidereal.

Ursa Minor, Ur Sam,
I, nor Pegasus
Peg as us, Orion,

Or I
On constellation cons
Tell at ion dignitaries.

Dig'nit Aries singles
Bar cooled singles' bar coo
Led dig it, sex, changed
Digits exchanged.

Zo, Di acted zodiac tedium
I, umbra, brace celestial
Lest I allow lowbrow browsing,
Singe erotica rot I, Castor storied,
I edify if you're our ethereality,

Mythic Kaleidoscope, My Thick Ale I Do Scope

The reality flaming flam in grafted
Rafted sojourn eying rest or edit
So journeying restored it.

Prep-aid, pre-paid,
PR-eyed, I'd preyed on id,
Once cenobite/no bite
Past elaborators.

Paste labor: a torso odalisk
Dali's kitsch, its charm armor
Or soothing soot
Hinging ingratiating rat,
I, a tinged Eden denier
I erased a sedated at edgy gyres
Residual model overcome patient.

I, dual mode lover, come pat,
I entitle it leisurely.

I surely revamp re vamp Electras,
Elect rash hoed Oedipus harrows.
I push arrows, comp lexicons
Complex I console.

Olé toreador, to read or
To re-adore either
I therapist, a pistoleer
O, leer.

Mythic Kaleidoscope, My Thick Ale I Do Scope

✴ As per asper gum my gummy
Fluorescent flu ore scent
Mica mic, a mild ew mildew
Sortie sort, i.e., phlegmatic phlegm
At Icarian, arian pastoral past oral
Fluid flu, I'd, yes, chewy eschew
Quaking qua king megalomania.

Me, gal, O man
I: a hero in heroin smug glee,
Smuggle "ear medicine."

Armed, I cinema macho chow-hound,
Who undid idle leisure, I, sure
Flush flu shivered.

I've red nose, gay,
Nosegay acute,
A cute ascent a scent
Fun kier vat I clean
Funkier vatic lean
Than a top sis thanatopsis
Windowed wind owed
Hum bleaching humble aching.

Hell as Hellas Hera mended
Her amended
Mayhem lode feathers
May hem, lo, defeat
Her sin tent intent.

Campus camp,
Us Pan tier aid pantie raid
Onlookers on lookers
Beam in or zoom.

Be a minor zoomorphic
Orphic leg end legend?
Singled sing-led
For Euridice's fore ur id
Ices do omens doom.

Enslaving laving washer:
Was her, your yo, ur call
I ope Calliope?

Her a Hera inferior
Infer I or Iowa's Io
Was cowed
Co-wed youthen you then
Her me's Hermes typewriter type
Writer keys toned keystoned Pluto
Crating plutocrating char on Charon.

Mythic Kaleidoscope, My Thick Ale I Do Scope

Circ. ean Circean mons trance
Monstrance conversions con versions
Chic kenosis chicken O, sis,
The sis thesis amuses
A muse sat hens Athens co-op coop

Fatalist's Fat A-Lists

Alphabet's alpha bets
The me theme
Pitchpipe pitch
Pipe at one A-tone:

Abashed, a bashed
Bar rages' barrages
Can dent candent
Donations; do nations
End or see endorsee
Flag on flagon?

Go sling gosling
Hat red hatred
In do or indoor
Jackanapes jack an ape's
K.O. a la koala
Lace rated lacerated
Massacres mass acres.
Needled need led
Onuses on uses
Peasants peas ants
Question quest I on
Ripply rip ply
Seamy sea my
Teething tee thing.
Urchin ur chin
Van ward vanward

War dens wardens,
Xy, lose xylose?
You then youthen
Zip per zipper.

❄ Do we, led, doweled pinheads, pin heads?
Do Zen's dozens seethe, contemplate see the con template?
Do vet-ailed dovetailed joint weeds join tweeds?
Do used doused conflagrations con flag rations?
Do tingly dotingly clear-cut clear cut trees urge on tree surgeon handiwork's hand-I works?
Do sage dosage needlings need ling's cod ex codex?
Do O.R. door menage men age?
Do nuts do-nuts plea sure pleasure?
Do nor donor skinflints skin flints?
Do native donative dowagers do wagers?
Do minion dominion alternatives alter natives?
Do me dome palaces Pa laces pal aces manage man age?
Do main domain watchdogs watch dogs?
Do geared dog-eared books tack book stack?
Do cent docent pennywise guys pen NY wiseguys advice ad vice to advise toad vise novices: No Vices!??

Charlatan
Char lat, an
Opinion
O pin I on
The me
Theme
So lip sis, tic
Solipsistic
Thesis
The sis
Pen chant
penchant
Agreed.

A greed
Conjoint
Con joint
Camaraderie
Cam, a rad, Erie
Lackawanna
Lack, a wanna-
Being,
Be in-
grained
Rained
Intractability.

In tract ability
The sis
Thesis
Tract I on
Traction
Assigned
As signed
Litany
Lit, any
Endorsee
End or see
Saw buck
Sawbuck
Of ten
Often
Dollared
Doll a red
Bill owing
Billowing
Flag. Rant
Flagrant
Opinion
O pin I on
Theme:
The me.

Fatalist fat, a list:
The me theme
The sis thesis
A pot he O sis apotheosis
The Archies thearchies
The or-ist theorist
A verse averse
A version aversion
The ism theism
A theism atheism
The Ma tic thematic
The O pathetic theopathetic
The or em theorem
The O sophist theosophist
The saurus thesaurus
The tic thetic
The ur gist theurgist
The rapist therapist
A side aside
A broadside abroad side
A do ado
A mending amending a men amen
A nab a sis anabasis
A nag ram anagram
An arch ism anarchism
An at he Ma anathema
An I'm ism animism

An I'm us animus
A prior I a priori
A ria aria
A scent ascent
A spiring aspiring
A script I on ascription
A toning atoning
A trophy atrophy
A venue avenue
A vast avast.

Fatalist's Fat A-Lists

❋   Threesome three so me,
Bigamist big,
A mist art
If ice artifice
For mat I've formative mendicant mend.

I can't man a kin manakin.
Ragamuffin
Rag a muffin ram I form.

Ramiform tomahawk to Ma hawk
Another a not her vanilla van.

I'll a tort I'll a tortilla can did ate.
Candidate end or see
Endorsee dubitable dub it able
In tole rant intolerant
Dish on or dishonor getaway.

Get a way, yak.
I'm a Yakima emblem a tic
Emblematic decor at or decorator disc
On tent discontent? No.
I some noisome oxidate ox I date
Or din ate ordinate soared.

So a red cab an A cabana sat.
Is factory statisfactory, punitive?
Pun it, I've artichoke art I choke.

A polo gist apologist ant, I matter.
Antimatter in do or indoor
Gymnosperm gym.

No sperm met
A physical metaphysical par
A graph paragraph man I cure.

Manicure xy lop honed
Xylophoned son at a sonata disc.

Our aged, discouraged badminton
Bad mint on Uranus.

Ur an us wallaby wall
A by centigrade cent I grade
Cusp id or cuspidor.

Carapace car a pace ant
I dote.

Antidote medulla me
Dull a me no pause
Menopause swords wall
Owing swordswallowing palookas.

Pa, look as male fact
Or malefactor masturbated mast
Ur bated mememto me men
To prop a gate propagate.

Quadrillion qua drill, I
On trigo
No me
Try trigonometry artifactor art
I, fact or myth O lo gist mythologist,
Investigate.

In vest, I gate gladiator
Glad I at
Or mathematics mat
Hem a tic's rag
A muff in ragamuffin dish
On or able dishonorable championship.

Champ, I on ship comp ass,
I on compassion, no net.
He less, nonetheless nonunion,
No nun, I
On significant sign.

If I can't prop it
I ate propitiate art I
Fact or artifactor gene rat
I on generation taxonomy.

Tax on O my panorama
Pan or ram a notation. Not at I
On anticipative antic I pat
I've figurative fig ur at I've palliative pall.

I, at I've identified.

I dent I fied ex
Per I, mentalist experimentalist,
Rein vent I on reinvention.

Fatalist's Fat A-Lists

   Pen tag, ram a tic
pentagramatic

Trip art it I on
Tripartition

Disc rim in at or
Discriminator

A bra cad a bra
Abracadabra

A pot he O sis
Apotheosis

Beat. If I, cat, I on
Beatification

The REM in Theremin

❋   Abandon a band on a bra, cad.
A bra abracadabra a la presto
Redacted a lap, restored, acted
The REM in theremin awe
At her aweather
Lingerie linger, i.e.
A nun strapped
A nun's trapped
An unstrapped
Abatement.

O, abate men to Cadillac cad;
I'll, acme me, wax you waxy.

Ouija board, I jab oar
Dalliances' alliance, sculled culled
Prognostic pro gnostic revelations revel at.

I, onshore horehound, hound
As underwearing asunder,
We a ring for mat form
At bust our bus tour pleasure.

Plea, sure, begin
Beg in gin fizz-led
Fizzled case, mate
Casemate ram parts
Ramparts for tresses fortresses.

The REM in Theremin

But tresses buttresses, carefree, care
Free the me theme bra in brain
Together to get her the REM in theremin
A band on abandon
Spell b-o-u-n-d spellbound.

Amiss, a miss adumbrated
A dumb rated aga in Asia.

Again as I, a liturgist, lit
Ur gist polemics, pole mics'
Antipathetic mass creeds.

Anti-Pa thetic, Ma's screeds
Against aga in staid aid
Istanbul rushes.

Is tan bulrushes' taint stain
Tantamount ant a mount
To urn eyed tourneyed
Hadj ousting?

Had jousting for mic formic acid
A Cid ant agonist antagonist awe?

Some awe's omelet let egg
Headstones, egghead's tones
Anear an ear feed back aversion.

Feedback: A version
The REM in theremin sonata son
At a bombardon tuba, leveraged.

Bombard on? Tubal Eve
Raged or a to Rio oratorio
Orchestrated or chest rated.

The REM in Theremin

Mushroomed mush roomed,
Or chard's orchards orbit
Or bit or ate orated in din ordeals.

Or deals, the or-ist theorist
Therein order by or allots
Imposed the rein or derby.

Oral lots I'm posed at testing attesting
An us anus a trophy ordure
SS atrophy or duress imp roved.

Improved, the or-ist theorist or a Tory oratory
Avers a vers rumor, rum or
Fur or furor, tail or tailor prose cut or
Prosecutor bargains.

Bar gains increased orange lair
In creased or angel air pantheistic
Pant heist icicling.

I cling or a pro nob is ora pro nobis
A stigma tic pin keyed
Astigmatic, pink-eyed,
Peers into peer sin to me.

At pieties' meat pie tie,
Sex changes exchanges transact.

Ex-changes, trans act along

A long drag show primadonna
Drags how prim a donna can-can can
Can humor hum or
Legitimate leg.

It I mate:
Meteor mete or measure
Me a sure theorist
The or-ist rat, I, fied ratified.

The REM in Theremin

The sis thesis
Parenthesis parent (he)
Sis denounces.
Den ounces of fish (offish odor)
OD or underpants
Hamper fumes
Under pant sham perfumes infuse
In fuse bomb as tic
Bombastic his to id
Histoid thesis.

Metastatic, the sis met
A static, pathetic Pa.

The tic he (manicured he-man, I)
Cured via led vialed anticipation antic.

I (pat I)
On my co-logical mycological support
Sup (Port, Stilton)
Stilt on wavering wave
Ringling Brothers ling broth
Ersatz at zany anybody's bodyshop repairs.

Hop rep airs farther fart her (fat her)
Father parent (he, tical coins urgently)
Parenthetical, co-insurgently remarks.

REM arks awake a wake
Dish on or dishonor his Tory history.

All Us I've Allusively Lyre Recited, Cited

Infer no Inferno can
On canon lodestar
Lode star lodes tar:

One time O net I, me
On going ongoing myth rough
My through the me theme Midi mid
I foundation found at I on
My's elf myself
Astumbling as tumbling
In to in toad ark woo'd
A dark wood.

All Us I've Allusively Lyre Recited, Cited

Iago, I, a golem lemon
On penchant meter
Pen chant me
Teratological at
O, logical demon demo nemesis
Emesis who said who's
Aid first water firs twater's
Able sable buckram buck
Ram tup per wary tupper
War your yo ur Ma id maid
Sinewed sin ewe dot: Othello.

Hello Des ire desire
De sire be a strapping
Doublebacking beast rapping double
Backing bow-legged bowl egged lay.

Off lay-off rest,
I've, restive, importuned.

Imp or tuned astringent,
A string entitled it, led,
Implied imp lied I'm plied.

✹ Onto logical ontological
Ontogenesis.

On to Genesis
Begin beg:

In the (me theme)
Beginning (beg inning)
There (the re:)
Was the (wast he)
Word (age wordage)
And (ante andante)
The (me theme)
Word (blind Alex, I a par rot word-blind alexia parrot)
Was (her washer)
God (own go-down)
And (roster one androsterone)
The (me theme)
Word (i.e. stripped wordiest, ripped)
Was (sailing wassailing)
With (standing withstanding)
God (evil go-devil).

Fare Well, Farewell

Into X, I, cant-intoxicant influent
In fluent slogan
Slog an us age usage
The me theme does press.

O, do espresso cart
Elite cartel iterations
Ration shot hot dosages?

Do sages' binges bin gestes testify?
Test if you lipogram OULIPO
Grammar marines in esteem teem
Abound a bound motto mot to avoid A Void.

Gram grammar maraud it or auditor types typeset
Ethereal here a la mode Alamo defeats, feats.

PR ivy, privy to can a Dada shout
Canada dash outhouse or gander
By house organ derby parlays par,
Lays its wayside allocations.

It sways ideal locations to prevent
Top rev entropy.

Ropy divertissement
A-styles divert.

Is semen tasty?
Lesser serendipities end.

Fare Well, Farewell

I, pities amass, am assoiled, oiled
An ointment anointment pries the priest,
He who led whole diagnostic consciences.
I, agnostic, con science's mythic kale
My thick ale new sand news and re-
Creation recreation in foreign info reign
(Rum or rumor writ, he'd writhed,
"We're readying a dying ozone O zone")
All us, I've, allusive fatalist, fat
A list A-list.

I'm a gist imagist
Your yo ur thesis the sis thesis
The REM in theremin fare
Well, farewell

The Me Theme.

Doug Nufer is the author of the poetry collections *We Were Werewolves* (Make Now, 2008), *The Dammed* (ubu.com, 2011), and *Lounge Acts* (Insert Blanc, 2013). His novels include *Lifeline Rule* (Spuyten Duyvil, 2015), *By Kelman Out of Pessoa* (Les Figues, 2011), *The Mudflat Man/The River Boys* (soultheft records, 2006), *On the Roast* (Chiasmus, 2004), *Negativeland* (Autonomedia, 2004), and *Never Again* (Black Square, 2004). He sells wine in Seattle.

Photo by Peggy Sullivan.

Parts of *The Me Theme* have appeared in *The Monarch Review*, *Make It True: Poetry from Cascadia* (Leaf Press), and *Verbivoracious Festschrift Volume 6: The Oulipo*. I'm grateful to the editors of those publications and especially grateful to Royce Becker, Jacob Smullyan, Annalisa Pesek, Daniel Levin Becker, and James Siena for helping me make this book.